Making
Marriage
Magnificent

365 Keys to Happiness

Reed & Lorena Markham

First Printing: August 1997

International Standard Book Number:

0-88290-613-5

Horizon Publishers' Catalog and Order Number:

2073

Printed and distributed in the United States of America by

Horizon
Publishers

& Distributors, Incorporated
P.O. Box 490 Bountiful, Utah 84011-0490

Table of Contents

❀ ❀ ❀ ❀ ❀ ❀ ❀ ❀

Introduction

In the following pages 365 tips and suggestions have been compiled on how to create and maintain a lasting and wonderful marriage. These tips include advice gathered from parents and grandparents, friends, church leaders, marriage experts and famous people. Each thought will direct you toward making your marriage magnificent!

The dictionary describes "magnificent" as "splendid, grand, excellent in quality." When we say "magnificent" we are referring to how marriage partners can feel great about themselves, their companion, their marriage and their relationships.

Many years ago Reed's father, John Markham, helped Brigham Young University design a sign for the entrance to the institution. Inscribed on the sign are the following words: "Enter to learn, go forth to serve." We hope that as you begin to read each chapter that your desire will be to take these suggestions and use them. Acting on many of these tips will help your marriage to be happy, healthy and magnificent!

Each strategy in this book takes less than a minute to read, yet every tip can have a great impact on your marriage. Remember, out of small things can come that which is great. (1 Nephi 16:29)

We recommend that you a read a thought each day, think about it, and ponder how it fits into your marriage. Then discuss the suggestion with your companion, decide if you're going to use it, and then make a commitment to apply it to your marriage.

One of the major reasons why some marriages have problems and fall apart is the failure of the marriage partners to work at their marriage. In today's fast-paced, high-tech society where the average American worker is spending more time at work and less time at home, the marriage relationship can easily be set aside or even forgotten. Lack of time is a problem for many Latter-day Saint couples trying to juggle work, children, church callings, community activity, and their marriage relationship. We have found that by using a focused approach to building marriage, minute-by-minute and action-by-action, both short- and long-term results can be attained.

Working on a marriage can begin with just one person—you. Start where you are and begin applying the advice found in each chapter. We suggest that you take out your calendar, planner, or a notebook and schedule a marriage tip each day. Use those minutes you have available each day to develop a happy, growing and magnificent marriage.

Defining a Great Marriage
❀ ❀ ❀ ❀ ❀ ❀ ❀ ❀

1

"There is no greater happiness than is found in the most meaningful of all human relationships: the companionship of husband and wife and parents and children."
— Gordon B. Hinckley

2

"A successful marriage requires falling in love many times, always with the same person."
— Mignon McLaughlin

3

"Next to the love between man and his Creator, the love of one man and one woman is the loftiest and the most illusive ideal that has been set before the world. A perfect marriage is like a pure heart; those who have it are fit to see God."
— Elizabeth Stuart Phelps

4

"Marriage can be difficult and discordant, and frustrated marriages are common. Yet real and lasting happiness is possible and marriages can be more of an exultant ecstasy than the human mind can conceive. This is within the reach of every couple, every person."
— Spencer W. Kimball

5

"Approach marriage with the lofty view it merits."

— David O. McKay

6

"Let every husband speak with respect, kindness, and appreciation for his wife. Let every wife look for and speak of the virtues of her husband."

— Gordon B. Hinckley

7

"Let husband and wife never speak in loud tones to each other unless the house is on fire."

— David O. McKay

8

"Foster home ties by continued companionship."

— David O McKay

9
Remember to put your marriage first.

10
"More and more families, even nations, if built upon secular sand instead of gospel granite, will suffer." — Neal A. Maxwell

11
"The greatest blessing in marriage is that it lasts so long. The years, like the varying interests of each year, combine to buttress and enrich each other. Out of many shared years, one life. In a series of temporary relationships, one misses the ripening, gathering, harvesting joys, the deep, hard-won truths of marriage."
— Richard C. Cabot

12

"Love is not blind. It sees more, not less. But because it sees more, it is willing to see less."

— Julius Gordon

13

"Good family life is never an accident, but always an achievement by those who share it."

— James H. Bossard

14

"One can be selfish and married. One can be married and happy. One could even be selfish and happy, to an extent, before marriage. But one can never remain married and remain selfish and be happy at the same time. Marriage is a thing you've got to give your whole mind to."

— Henrik Ibsen

15

"Except a man and his wife enter into an everlasting covenant and be married for eternity, while in this probation, by the power and authority of the Holy Priesthood, they will cease to increase when they die; that is, they will not have any children after the resurrection."

— Joseph Smith

16

"I am concerned about family life in the Church. We have wonderful people, but we have too many whose families are falling apart. It is a matter of serious concern. I think it is my most serious concern."

— Gordon B. Hinckley

17

"The Christian home is the Master's workshop where the processes of character molding are silently, lovingly, faithfully, and successfully carried on."
— Lord Houghton

Building Spirituality

❊ ❊ ❊ ❊ ❊ ❊ ❊ ❊

18
Remember that marriage is a covenant, not a contract.

19
Help and support each other in magnifying your individual church callings.

20
Remember, there can be no exaltation without eternal marriage.

21

Discuss together things that are keeping you away from Heavenly Father. Take steps to eliminate them from your life.

22

Keep your eye on the big picture. Don't be overcome by the latest parade of events in your daily life.

23

If you live close enough, attend the temple together at least monthly. If you don't have a temple recommend, spend time on the temple grounds and in the visitor's center to feel the Spirit.

24

Be worthy of a temple recommend. Discuss your worthiness at least once a year with your companion and your bishop.

25

Do service projects as a couple. The world is full of opportunities to serve. Begin with your own neighborhood.

26

Plan to serve a mission together when you retire. Make submitting mission papers a part of your retirement strategy.

27

Remember that a worthy priesthood holder governs his home in love and is prepared to give priesthood blessings when necessary.

28

Work together to develop personal histories for yourself, your parents and the members of your family. Spend time every month on your genealogy and become familiar with the local family history center.

29

Follow the counsel of our current prophet. Read and study the Prophet's messages in Church magazines, books, and speeches. Listen to General Conference and read the conference *Ensigns*.

30

Study the advice and counsel of the prophet and other church leaders on marriage and family.

31

Search the scriptures for advice and help in your marriage and personal relationships.

32

Share your marriage and family plans with Heavenly Father. Be specific as you pray.

33

Instill the desire to serve a mission and to be married in the temple in your children by example, by personal prayer, by regular family home events, and by making these goals a continuing topic of discussion.

34

Study the scriptures as a family, and memorize favorite passages.

35
Ask yourself, "Is the love of Christ in my home?" Act upon your answer.

36
Memorize the Articles of Faith as a family and make them the foundation of your religious beliefs.

37
Memorize and sing church hymns together.

38
Place a picture of an LDS temple in a prominent location in your home.

39
Place marriage pictures in a prominent location in your home. Look at them often.

40
As a husband, magnify your role as priesthood leader. As a wife, support your husband.

41
Avoid pride. Be humble. Selfishness leads to selfish decisions.

42
Avoid movies, videos, and television shows which devalue marriage covenants.

43

Share inspirational thoughts and quotes with your companion often.

44

Make lists of key ideas you learn from General Conference. You will always learn something that will better yourself and your marriage.

45

Subscribe to the church magazines and use them in your home. Read, especially, the articles dealing with marriage.

46
Share your testimony with your spouse and family at least once a month.

47
Do temple sealings or initiatory ordinances around your anniversary date to remind you of your eternal covenants.

48
Attend your Sunday Meetings regularly together. If church callings pull you in different directions, try still to spend a few moments together on the Sabbath.

49
Fast together on fast Sundays.

50
Fast for help in dealing with difficult problems.

51
Selfishness leads away from the Spirit and from each other. Avoid pride. Be humble.

52

Love is a powerful tool for bringing an inactive or non-member spouse into the church. Try:

— having family home evening.
— working on your own spirituality.
— avoiding defensiveness.
— teaching your children the gospel.
— sharing your testimony.
— playing church hymns.

Enhancing Communication

53

Speak words of appreciation and encouragement daily. Use phrases such as: "Thank you," "I'm proud of you," "You make me happy," "You're strong," etc.

54

Compliment your mate daily—"your hair looks great," "your smile makes me feel terrific," etc.

55

A deaf husband and a blind wife are always a happy couple. — Danish proverb

56

Deal with little hurts as they come. Don't let molehills become mountains.

57

Don't forget to kiss each other good-bye when leaving for work. At the end of the day, share a big welcoming bear hug and a kiss.

58

Love is always saying you're sorry when you've done or said something wrong.

59

Share the details of your time apart. Discuss your experiences at home and at work.

60

In heated discussions, use phrases that calm anger such as: "I make mistakes, too," and "Forgive me."

61
Turn off the television or radio and have a long, quiet talk together.

62
Have lofty dreams but realistic expectations.

63
Send clear messages when you speak, and say what you mean.

64
Be willing to compromise.

65

When feeling angry, count to ten before you speak.

66

Tell your companion often that you are glad you married him or her.

67

Respect your mate's privacy. Everyone needs space and solitude.

68

If the emotion of anger is a factor in your life, learn and sing church hymns daily.

69

Create an atmosphere of being open to discussion by looking at your spouse during conversations, turning off the television, and eliminating noisy distractions.

70

If you are angered by a wrong done you by another, lean not toward remembering it, but toward forgiving it.

71

The average American watches television for 7-9 hours a day. Limit the amount you watch. Talk to your mate instead.

72

Don't interrupt your spouse. Good conversation involves taking turns.

73

Don't contradict, comment on or change your spouse's message. Try to listen with complete understanding.

74

Let your partner know, in a constructive manner, if he or she does or says something that upsets or hurts you. Avoid negative words, phrases and labels. You can't throw mud without getting some of it on you.

75

Communicate your needs and wishes in a non-accusatory, non-demanding manner. Marriage is not a courtroom drama—leave prosecution and defense tactics alone.

76

Avoid faultfinding. J. Golden Kimball said: "If you can handle your own house and mind your own business, you will have no time for fault-finding."

77

Try to prevent misunderstandings. In a disagreement, remember that your spouse is not purposely trying to offend you—he or she just has a different view of things.

78

Value your companion's uniqueness. No two individuals are exactly the same. Each of us communicates through a frame of reference that is the sum of all our experiences, thoughts, and actions in life.

79

Encourage communication. A lack of communication can create a host of negative emotions such as fear, jealousy, anger, and hostility.

80

Identify problems you may have in your communication style. These might include not talking, pseudo listening, and ignoring your partner.

81

Carefully discern whether your spouse wants advice or just a listening ear.

82

Don't try to impose your viewpoint on your spouse. Be open-minded and value each other's free agency.

83

Be a reflective listener. Repeat statements that your companion makes to you to see if you understand the correct meaning.

84

Do not gossip about your spouse or your marriage. Value and protect your privacy.

85

Concentrate when you listen. Effective listening takes practice and careful focus.

86

The fool speaks, the wise man listens.
— Ethiopian proverb

87

Don't be judgmental. You are not the judge nor jury for every action your companion takes.

88

Examine your communication technique. It should be understandable, inspiring and uplifting.

89

Never criticize your partner. There is a big difference between hurtful criticism and a thoughtful, constructive discussion of life's experiences.

90

Never allow others to criticize your partner. Defend your companion with the facts.

91

When traveling together, use that time to plan and dream about the future.

92
Express your affection for your spouse every day in a variety of ways.

93
Buy and read together a book on building communication skills.

94
Express your affection in public but don't overdo it. Hold hands, put your arm around your mate.

95

Make use of good music, poetry, and literature to add a little romance to your marriage.

96

Speak kindly and with respect to your partner. Try not to say anything unkind or disrespectful all day long.

97

Don't raise your voice in discussions with your mate. The neighbors and children don't need to hear what you are saying.

98
Don't put down your mate in jest. It's much better to learn to laugh at yourself. Remember that those who learn to laugh at themselves never run out of things to laugh at.

99
Learn to understand your spouse's non-verbal communications. This includes facial expressions, posture, eye contact and actions.

100
Avoid the problem with most politicians. Think before you speak.

101

If you are angry, verbalize it to yourself. See if you can put into words why you are feeling the emotion.

102

Attack the problem, not your mate.

103

Use "I" statements rather than "you" statements. Say, "I feel upset when you don't take out the trash" rather than "you never take out the trash."

104

Express your expectations. Your companion can't read your mind, even if he or she knows you well.

105
Say, "I love you" to your companion daily.

106
Tell your mate one thing you like about him or her each day.

107
Go on a leisurely walk and talk. Go to a scenic park, to the beach or the mountains.

108
Share the chores. Doing the dishes or cleaning the yard is a great time to chat too.

109

Hold weekly and monthly planning and scheduling meetings with your spouse.

110

If you did not fully understand what your mate said, ask "Is this what you mean?"

111

"Listening can be a lively art in itself. You learn more by talking less and listening better than you might believe. But a good listener isn't one who just doesn't talk. A good listener listens, hears, reflects, comments."

-Elaine Cannon

112

Really look at your companion. Have you noticed how people don't look at each other these days?

113

Compliment your spouse both in private and in public. Compliment your companion in conversations with family and friends.

Solving Differences

❀ ❀ ❀ ❀ ❀ ❀ ❀

114

Discuss problems while eating a favorite food. Remember, "Just a spoonful of sugar helps the medicine go down."

115

Think about it: "A problem that is located and identified is already half solved!"
— R. Carlson

116

Did you know that when a married couple is walking down the street, the one three or four steps ahead usually is the one who is angry?

117

After an argument, don't hold grudges. Never let a dispute continue to tomorrow.

118

Handle your problems with a Christ-like approach. Ask yourself, "What would the Savior do?"

119

Ask your spouse for specific advice.

120

In dealing with problems, don't shut out your spouse. Be open.

121

Don't assume your position is always right or better. We live in an age of many solutions and possibilities.

122

Problem solving involves knowing how to solve the problem. Ralph Waldo Emerson once said: "I like people who can do things. When Edward and I struggled in vain to drag our big calf into the barn, the Irish girl put her finger into the calf's mouth and led her in directly."

123

In researching the solution to a problem you should listen to the advice of friends or relatives, but always follow the promptings of the Spirit before you make a decision.

124

Problems bring stress. By managing your stress through physical exercise, good nutrition and sharing with others, you will make better decisions.

125

Divorce doesn't solve all problems. If you don't work on the problems that are troubling you now in your marriage, it's 100% guaranteed that you will carry them into another marriage.

126

Remember that divorce is not part of the gospel plan. Commit with your spouse that you'll not try to make it the solution to your problems.

127

Compromise involves making sacrifices. Be willing to change for the better.

128

"Discovery (of a solution to a problem) consists of looking at the same thing as everyone else and thinking something different."

— Albert Szent-Gyorgyi

129

Have a clear perspective when solving problems. Step aside from the problem and look at the big picture.

130

Use a magnifying-glass approach to focus in on the problems. Identify key issues.

131
What marriage needs is more open minds and fewer open mouths.

132
Problem-solving involves a winning attitude.

133
Pick the best time to discuss your problems. Avoid Mondays, late nights and sleep-deprived moments.

134

"No matter how complicated a problem is, it usually can be reduced to a simple, comprehensible form which is often the best solution."
— An Wang

135

Discuss your problems in private. Many couples go into the bedroom and close the door behind them when they have a problem to discuss and resolve.

136

Problem-solving can be a growing experience. Life is a test.

137

Sometimes, for change to occur, you have to change first.

138

Seek counseling and professional help if you are dealing with serious problems such as abuse or drug dependency.

139

Brainstorm solutions. Write down lots of possibilities before you arrive at a decision.

140
Never go to bed angry, even if you have to lose a little sleep. If you can, agree to postpone the discussion of the problem.

141
Be conscious of forces that pull you apart, like long working hours, addiction to television, and shopaholism.

Learning About Your Spouse

❀ ❀ ❀ ❀ ❀ ❀ ❀

142

Don't expect your partner to do everything perfectly.

143

Pamper, and fuss over your companion sometimes. Make your spouse a king or queen for a day.

144

Make sure you recognize and respond when your mate needs a little extra love and attention.

145

Put your spouse first. When making important decisions such as vacation plans or large purchases, think about what your companion wants to do.

146

Your companion is a unique person. Don't compare him or her to anyone else.

147

"When one door of happiness closes, another opens; but often we look so long at the closed door that we do not see the one which has been opened for us." —Helen Keller

148

If your mate likes fragrant flowers, buy roses or gardenias.

149

Cut out items from magazines, bulletins, newspapers, and newsletters which are interesting or funny. Share them with your mate.

150

Remember what first attracted your spouse to you. Discuss this experience with your companion.

151

Apply the golden rule in your marriage. Do unto your companion as you would like your companion to do unto you.

152

Do something with your companion that you know he or she will appreciate, even if its something you don't usually enjoy. For example, watch a football game or shop at the mall together.

153

Make a list of his or her favorite things. Refer to it often when choosing things to eat, do or buy.

154

Copy his or her favorite songs onto a tape for special listening and sharing.

155

Ask each other philosophical questions about values, attitudes, and feelings. For example, "Do you think that spouses ought to tell each other everything? Why? Why not?"

156
Give your spouse an article, magazine, or book about his or her hobby such as gardening, gourmet cooking, or crafts.

157
Do the little things your mate appreciates. Set the table, take out the trash.

158
Cancel that after-work meeting or civic event and spend the time with your companion.

159
Share a spiritual moment with your spouse. Retell a favorite story or experience.

160

Play a guessing game. Guess your spouse's favorite color, sport, t.v. show, etc.

161

Bring home your partner's favorite food item, movie rental, magazine, etc.

162

Ask yourself, "Have I done any good to my companion today?"

163

Love takes time to grow, which means you ought to love your spouse more with the passage of time.

164

What are the qualities you look for in a friend? Cultivate the qualities that will make you your spouse's best friend.

165

If you are walking or sitting outside and it gets cold, rub noses like the Eskimos.

Sharing Surprises

❀ ❀ ❀ ❀ ❀ ❀ ❀

166
"Carpe diem!" This is Latin for "seize the moment!" Think of a creative way to give your companion a romantic surprise.

167
Bring your spouse his or her favorite candy bar, chocolate truffles, jelly beans, or red licorice.

168

A hug a day keeps the frowns away. And try ten-second kisses!

169

Give your partner a gift of music; a CD or a tape, or, learn a song with a musical instrument. Arrange for an at-home concert.

170

Send your mate a card or telegram that says, "I love you."

171

Send a message, card, or postcard to your spouse every day when you are away on trips.

172
Always give cards to your companion on special occasions, but also give cards at other times to show you care.

173
Call your mate just to say, "I love you."

174
Write and mail your spouse a love letter.

175
Woo and wow your companion with flowers.

176
Put together a list of things your companion will love. Do one a week.

177

Arrange all the details of a secret date. Don't say where you are going. Try something very different from your usual dates.

178

Leave love, appreciation, and encouragement notes in unexpected places such as in a book your spouse is reading.

179

Surprise your mate with a small hidden gift in the car, wallet, etc.

180

Make a treasure hunt leading your spouse to a special gift.

181

Record a message for your mate. Express your feelings, recite poetry, sing!

182

Save up extra money for something exotic, like a helicopter ride, or a scuba diving trip.

183

Send flowers with a special message. For example, send sunflowers if you want to send the message: "you are the sunshine of my life."

184
Compose a poem for your companion.

185
Recreate a special occasion: your first date, when you got engaged, your wedding night.

186
Give gifts, candies, notes, cards, and messages to your spouse, to be opened each day he or she is away.

187
Send a birthday card for every week of your companion's birthday month.

188
Plan a theme-night dinner. How about a Hawaiian luau? Don't forget the Hawaiian music, scenic posters and some coconuts.

189
Send a whole bunch of birthday cards, all at once, to your companion.

190

Be creative when planning your dates. Plan some dates that will be remembered for a lifetime.

191

Call and arrange to bring dinner home.

192

Tape something humorous in a place he or she will read it.

193

Every day for a week (or a month) share a different reason why you love your mate.

Finding Variety

❀ ❀ ❀ ❀ ❀ ❀ ❀

194
Keep your courtship alive by doing something loving for your companion every day.

195
Steadily work on gathering food, clothing and other essentials for your food storage.

196
Exercise daily with your companion by jogging, swimming, or doing aerobics.

197

Have a second honeymoon. It doesn't have to be expensive or even long distance. Research some romantic getaways in your area.

198

Buy a large puzzle with lots of pieces. Put the puzzle in an out-of-the-way place. Spend time working together to solve it.

199

Learn a new skill, craft or sport. Expand your knowledge and ability.

200

Take a class together at the local college or community center. Take a class that will be interesting and fun, like painting, dancing, or even karate.

201

Rub your spouse's back, neck or feet. This is particularly appreciated after an exhausting day.

202

Show your love by touching each other frequently. Give lots of hugs, pats and squeezes.

203
Keep your minds active. Find a crossword puzzle in the newspaper. Work together with the dictionary to solve it.

204
Get tickets to a favorite event like a volley-ball game or the theater.

205
Make a list of places you'd like to travel to. Make realistic plans to visit each place.

206
Have a private film festival. Rent a stack of your favorite movies and buy snacks to share.

207
Try some new activities: miniature golfing, white-water rafting, biking, bowling, or horse-back riding.

208
Go to a museum or planetarium.

209
Share your dreams and desires.

210
Go to an amusement park.

211
Drive past beautiful homes in your area.

212
Take lots of pictures during your trips.

213
Put together news events from your date of marriage. Include them in a marriage history scrapbook.

214
Brainstorm things that can make your marriage better. Discuss and do them.

215
Take short trips together. A romantic weekend getaway is great therapy!

216

Learn how to say "I love you" in several languages—

> Spanish- Te amo
> French- Je t' aime
> Japanese- Ai shite imasu
> Swedish- Jag alskar dig
> German- Ich liebe dich
> Hawaiian- Aloha wau ia oe

217

Read marriage-enriching books.

218

Enroll in seminars or workshops on marriage.

219

Start a new hobby together such as doing crafts, making pottery, or collecting stamps and rocks.

220

You don't need a special reason to celebrate. You can even celebrate the sun rising or setting.

221
Follow our church leaders' advice and go on a date once a week (without the children).

222
Go to a garden or arboretum.

223
When working through hard schedules, relax for a while by taking a quick trip to a beach, a park, an arboretum, or to a zoo.

224

Compile a history of your marriage. Set a specific date and time each month to work on it.

225

Make sure you have variety in your date-night activities. Pick a new date each week. This week go to a movie, next week, have a picnic.

226

Make an ordinary day extraordinary. Make his or her special dessert on that day.

227

Take turns planning a complete date. Surprise your mate.

228

Work together. Do the laundry together. Help each other with chores.

229

Create a new family tradition.

230

Arrange for a babysitter and go out to a movie.

231

Explore the back roads and out-of-the-way places in your area. Enjoy just being together.

232

Reward yourselves on a regular basis for making progress toward a special long-term goal.

Financing Your Future
❀ ❀ ❀ ❀ ❀ ❀ ❀

233
Live within your means. Spend less than you receive.

234
Be realistic in your financial expectations.

235
Pay your tithing. Blessings will follow.

236

Discuss your ideas about earning and spending money for the present and for the coming year.

237

Make a budget and keep it. Know what your monthly spending plan is before the month begins.

238

Set aside funds in your budget for items each of you would like to purchase.

239
Don't go shopping when you don't have money to spend.

240
Separate your needs from your wants.

241
Begin your retirement and estate plans. Talk with an investment counselor. Prepare a will or other documents with legal counsel.

242
Enroll in a financial workshop. Check books out of the library on financial management.

243

Less-expensive flowers can be bought from supermarkets and street vendors.

244

Some say that a model marriage is one in which the wife is the treasure and the husband the treasury.

245

Buy gifts on sale and save them for future special occasions.

246

Plan for necessities first.

247
Teach your children how to make money decisions and how to save money.

248
Pay your debts promptly. Have a system for tracking them and specify days of the month for paying bills.

249
Exercise control in spending.

250

Cut up your credit cards and throw them away unless you're able to pay them off every month.

251

Get as much education and training as possible.

252

Have life, medical, car, and home insurance.

253

Put a certain amount of your earnings into a savings account.

254

Work towards owning your own home.

255

Vacation in the off-season or wait for a good deal. A vacation package might be better than paying for items such as plane tickets and hotel tickets separate, but examine it closely. Be cautious of "sweepstakes" and contests offering free trips.

256

Keep accurate financial records. If you have a computer, buy and utilize a good family finance program.

257
Wait until you have the money to buy items. Don't get tangled in high interest rates.

258
Donate used items to Deseret Industries or other charities. Keep detailed receipts for tax deductions.

259
Start a savings account toward something you both want, such as a romantic trip to Hawaii.

260

"We, as Latter-day Saints, are in sore need of a vision of the future which will uplift us above and beyond the petty, sordid interests of the moment . . . It is riches, automobiles, oriental rugs, fashion, social functions, class distinction, and other worldly things that appeal to our covetousness more than just doing right, for they are advertised better and have a stronger appeal to our sordid natures."

—J. Golden Kimball

Reaching Your Highest Potential

❀ ❀ ❀ ❀ ❀ ❀ ❀

261
Remember that having a successful marriage is more than finding the right person. It's also a matter of being the right person.

262
"Do it now."

—Spencer W. Kimball

263
Constantly improve yourself. Remember, we grow line upon line.

264
Make the commitment to be a magnificent marriage partner throughout your lifetime.

265
"A good marriage must be created. It is doing things for each other, not in the attitude of duty or sacrifice, but in the spirit of joy."
—Wilfred A. Peterson

266
Nothing makes a marriage rust like distrust.

267
Focus on the good times in your marriage.

268
"Lengthen your stride."   — Spencer W. Kimball
Decide how you can "lengthen your stride" in your marriage, and then do it.

269
Even if your spouse is unwilling, you can strengthen your marriage by improving yourself.

270
"All things are possible until they are proved impossible—even the impossible may only be so, as of now."
— Pearl S. Buck

271
Be gentle, kind and courteous.

272
Control your thoughts. Be pro-active, not re-active.

273

Stay healthy together by living the Word of Wisdom, and having regular medical check-ups.

274

Be mature. Put away "childish things" and attitudes.

275

Have a sense of humor. Laughing prevents hardening of the attitudes.

276

Have you noticed how time seems to be passing quicker? President Kimball urged the Saints to "quicken their step." Have you "quickened your step" in trying to accomplish your marriage goals?

277

Allow each other some "personal time" to pursue special interests.

278

Take time to make yourself attractive for your spouse.

279
Expect good things in your marriage while you are working to better it. You'll be surprised at the outcome.

280
Don't worry. Be happy.

281
Be sensitive, modest, caring, and giving.

282
Don't confuse possessiveness with love.

283
Be hopeful. Great experiences are coming your way.

284
Do not keep a tally of wrongs committed against you.

285
Your love is either growing or withering. Cultivate and nourish it.

286
Find a marriage you admire. Make a plan for acquiring the good traits of that marriage.

287
Use a calendar or planner to keep track of your busy life. Failing to plan is planning to fail.

288
Don't forget to use common courtesies, such as saying thank you and excuse me, and opening doors and letting your companion go in first.

289
Save mementos of places you've visited together. Enjoy remembering by putting them on the refrigerator, for a time.

290
Exercise at least 20 minutes a day.

291
Be determined to be cheerful. Your happiness in life depends more upon your inner attitude than your outward circumstances.

292
Endure your trials. These tests will help you grow. Take them a day, an hour, or a minute at a time, as necessary.

293
Do not use love as an excuse to coerce favors.

294
Be courteous, attentive, kind and considerate.

295

Have a positive attitude. The cup is half full, not half empty.

296

Persevere. Never give up on your problems without consulting with Heavenly Father and following his guidance.

297

Write in a journal regularly. President Kimball recommended that every member keep a journal.

298
Mutual service makes for a happier marriage.

299
Don't forget that marriage is a give-and-take process.

300
Be optimists. Look for the good life together.

301

"I have always believed that a good laugh was good for both the mental and physical digestion."
— Abraham Lincoln

302

Write marriage goals down in your planner as constant reminders.

303

Read a book on time management.

304

Consider and live each day as if it were the most important day in your marriage.

305
"A person's character is but half-formed until after wedlock."   — Charles Simmons

306
Always give at least 100% to your marriage partnership.

307
Don't try to do too much. When you have too much on the platter, something is bound to fall off.

308
Make a list of things that would better your marriage and apply one each week. For example, "I won't complain this week."

309
Develop a family library of good books including church books and the classics.

310
"Be cheerful. Never complain. Have mutual confidence. Keep no secrets from one another and let no jealousy creep in."
— Amos Alonzo Stagg

311

List the qualities of an ideal home and do those which can be done in your home.

312

Be happy. Happiness is infectious.

313

Choose your friendships carefully. Don't let friends interfere with time with your companion.

314

Write down short- and long-term goals for your marriage. Review them monthly.

315

Improvement in marriage takes time. Do it little by little.

316

Making marriage work is like operating a farm. You have to start all over again each morning. — old Idaho proverb

317

Be willing to share yourself and your time with others.

318

Trust each other. Never let your partner down.

319
It is never too late to change. Changing yourself is repentance in action.

320
Reevaluate your schedule regularly and change it as necessary to make time for each other.

321
Share memories in quiet moments. Enjoy your past as well as your present and future.

322
Try new things. Keep your marriage fresh.

323
"A truly happy marriage is one in which a woman gives the best years of her life to the man who has made them the best."
—Eleanor Doan

Creating Forever Families

❀ ❀ ❀ ❀ ❀ ❀ ❀

324

"Foster home ties by continued companionship."
— David O. McKay

325

Accept the fact that changes will be needed
in your marriage. Adjust.

326

Do service projects as a family: serve food
at a homeless shelter, visit the elderly at a rest
home, go on a service scavenger hunt in your
local neighborhood.

327

Keep up the communication with children who have left the home by regular letters, phone calls and visits.

328

Call or send gifts on special occasions. Make a calendar of important family dates, especially birthdays and anniversaries.

329

"A real home is a picture of heaven on earth."
— Eleanor Doan

330
Though you become a parent, remember that you are still a companion.

331
Help your children be selective with their friends.

332
Discipline in the home is necessary. Find a method that works for your family.

333
Keep your priorities straight. Mom's main responsibility is effective mothering, not working outside the home.

334

Prepare your children to receive church ordinances such as baptism and priesthood advancements. Create important family celebrations for these events.

335

Praise children on a daily basis. Studies show that children receive over 200,000 negative messages at school before the age of 19. Counteract negativity with positive, specific praise.

336

Teach your children to read. Read good books to them daily, beginning when they are very young.

337

Keep close to your extended family.

338

Work together to make your home and yard a lovely place.

339

Respect your companion, and your children will do the same.

340

Plan the family schedule together with family members. Keep a family calendar. Don't forget to include special events important to individuals such as a little-league baseball game.

341

Care for your parents: welcome them to your home, help take care of their needs, and treat them with love and encouragement.

342

Teach your children values through example. This will make dealing with life's problems easier.

343
Have common goals as a family: spiritual, educational, physical, social, and financial.

344
Share in the discipline of children and support each other's decisions.

345
Sustain your church leaders, including your local leaders.

346
Have a personal interview with each member of the family on a regular basis.

347

Help children who have left the home when appropriate. Let them know you are there to back them up and encourage them.

348

Hold regular family reunions. Make them fun and memorable.

349

Develop a family newsletter.

350

Pray as a family both morning and night.

351
Great joy comes from having and raising children. Foster sweet, loving, eternal family ties.

352
Spend time with each child every day, even if it is only for a few minutes.

353
Have family rules and expect them to be honored and obeyed.

354
Make sure your children understand that you love them and are concerned for their well being. Tell them so often.

355
Show your children that you and your spouse love each other, both in words and actions.

356
Have the entire family contribute money or services for a project.

357
Teach the importance of work to children. Prepare them effectively for the world of work.

358
What would you like your children's marriages to be like? You are their marriage role models.

359
Write to the television networks expressing the need for more programs reflecting positive marriages and families.

360
Take the kids to a babysitter, and enjoy an at-home date. Dress up for the occasion. Have a nice dinner and even dance together.

361
Talk about the positive aspects of marriage with your associates and friends. Don't dwell on the negatives.

362
Build a good relationship with your in-laws by keeping them informed of your family, calling them and doing things with them.

363
Write to the editor of a local newspaper on the value of marriage.

364
"Marriage is a book in which the first chapter is written in poetry and the remaining chapters in prose."
— Beverly Nichols

365
Always remember that your marriage is eternal. Your goal is to bring yourself and all your family into the celestial kingdom, with not a soul lost.

& Distributors, Incorporated

Mailing Address:
P.O. Box 490
Bountiful, Utah 84011-0490

Street Address:
50 South 500 West
Bountiful, Utah 84010

Local Phone: (801) 295-9451
WATS (toll free): 1 (800) 453-0812
FAX: (801) 295-0196

Internet: www.horizonpublishers.com